WOLFGANG AMADEUS MOZART

PIANO CONCERTO No. 25

C major/C-Dur/Ut majeur
K 503

Ernst Eulenburg Ltd

London · Mainz · Madrid · New York · Paris · Prague · Tokyo · Toronto · Zürich

CONTENTS

PREFACE

If Johann Sebastian Bach may be thought of as the 'inventor' of the cembalo concerto, then to Wolfgang Amadeus Mozart goes the credit for having shaped the classical piano concerto. His concertos justifiably rank as great moments in solo music accompanied by orchestra, as a high point even in Mozart's own œuvre:

…it was only in the piano concertos that Mozart achieved his ideal. They are the peak of all his instrumental achievement, at least in the orchestral domain,

was on one occasion the judgement of Alfred Einstein.[1] To be sure, Mozart drew on predecessors and role models, such as Johann Christian Bach, for instance. From the latter's sonatas he created his three piano concertos, K107; other concertos were from piano compositions by other composers – preliminary exercises, compositional studies, so to speak. Then in 1773 in Salzburg he produced with the D major concerto, K175, the first work of his own. Composed up to 1791 were a total of 23 independent concertos (one of them for two pianos, one for three). Seven more were added to these including those arrangements of Bach's piano sonatas and the so-called 'pasticcio' concertos from sonata movements by other composers, together with two separate rondo movements as alternative finales.

Revolutionary innovations in instrumental construction prefigured the flowering of piano music in Viennese classicism. Thanks to the piano-hammer mechanism, touch and dynamics could be modified – opening now in the aftermath of the inflexible cembalo sound a vast world of interpretational diversity. And Mozart exploited it to show himself and his art in a favourable light. His piano concertos were written primarily for himself, being sometimes completed only shortly before the planned performance. So it is not surprising that solo parts were notated only cursorily and later added to or altered.

The Piano Concerto No.25 in C major, K503, is the first of the last three great concertos. If previously these *opera* had originated in relatively quick succession, they became less frequent in the last years of his life: after the C major concerto at the end of 1786, the 'Coronation' Concerto in D major, K537, then followed only in 1788, and in 1791, the year of his death, the B flat major work, K595. Strangely enough, though, Mozart made use of this form to present himself in subscription concerts as instrumental virtuoso; with 'academies' during the winter season and Lent he introduced himself to Vienna's influential classes as piano teacher and soloist for private concerts and was hence in a position to augment his earnings not inconsiderably. In addition, Mozart was at this time also attempting to establish himself as an opera composer. With the premiere of *Le Nozze di Figaro*, 1 May 1786, Mozart could here initially chalk up a decisive success with professionals, then also with the wider public. After that, whereas during the summer chamber music came to the fore, Mozart was then again concerned first of all with preparing the traditional winter academy concerts. A new piano concerto, namely that in C major, K503, was completed, and the composer entered it on 4 December 1786 into his *Verzeichnüß aller meiner Werke* as: 'a piano concerto. Accompaniment. 2 violins, 2 violas, 1 flute, 2 oboes, 2 bassoons, 2 French horns, 2 clarinets, timpani and bass'. Mozart had begun it, though, still earlier: the opening tutti, together with solo exposition, was already composed by March 1785.[2]

Four evenings were planned at first, so father Leopold reported to his daughter Nannerl on

[1] Alfred Einstein: *Mozart. His Character, His Work*, trans. Arthur Mendel and Nathan Broder (New York, 1965), 287

[2] See Alan Tyson: *Mozart. Studies of the Autograph Scores* (Cambridge/MA, London, 1987), 151f.

IV

8 December 1786; that is, Wolfgang would be giving: '4 Advent academies at the casino'.[3] However, planning the subscription concerts ended up in the background, for on 8 January 1787 Mozart unexpectedly travelled to Prague: 'Your brother and his wife must be in Prague by this time, for he wrote to say that he was leaving Vienna last Monday.'[4] After a three-year period 'without a symphony', Mozart had whipped up a new work, in D major, K504, the so-called 'Prague' symphony. Mozart remained several weeks and it seems that he wanted to establish there a second 'supporting leg'. The contract for a new opera was the fruit of this trip, and the composition of *Don Giovanni* was to take centre stage in his creative efforts for the year 1787. He could not even be bothered with the concerts at Lent as usual in Vienna that normally brought him material security. Interest in the piano concerto, a central genre in Mozart's works, waned.

Even though we have no direct evidence, we can assume that Mozart played the C major concerto for the first time in one of the four December academies in 1786, presumably on 5 December in the Trattner casino. That he finished it only shortly before the performance suggests the work pressure felt by the composer. Mozart must then have also taken the new composition along on the journey to Prague. Only a single performance, though, is documented. On the return trip from Potsdam to Vienna, Mozart gave on 12 May 1789 in the Leipzig Gewandhaus an academy in which he performed besides the B flat major concerto, K456, also that in C major. It was not printed in his lifetime; only in 1797 after long planning and at her own expense did the widow Constanze publish it herself. According to the title-page, it was dedicated to Prince Louis Ferdinand of Prussia.

The Piano Concerto in C major, K503, is Mozart's longest concerto (1st movement: 432 bars, 2nd movement: 109 bars, 3rd movement: 382 bars) and – like the works of this genre in general – in three movements. Virtuosic brilliance and balanced formal structure tie in stylistically with the concertos in A major, K488, and in C minor, K491. Yet the harmonic configuration, the continuous oscillation between major and minor, the witty dialoguing of solo and orchestra, the strong contrapuntal saturation, the frequent use of pedal point as well as the overflowing melodic abundance give the work a character all its own. Orchestration with paired oboes, bassoons and horns along with one flute – which Mozart no longer did without after the B flat major concerto, K450 – and the utilization of trumpets and timpani characteristic of a C-major concerto give the solo work a superb framework. (The violas are, incidentally, not *divisi*, as given in Mozart's *Verzeichnüß*.)

Commencing majestically, indeed almost like a march, is the *Allegro maestoso* that turns out formally to be an amalgamation of baroque ritornello technique and classical sonata-movement form. Right from the start, with chromaticism and darkening minor key, Mozart sets the course for a very smooth, fluent and harmonically iridescent elaboration. The repeatedly emerging three-quaver upbeat motif setting up the further course, likewise the counterpoint, already indicates the canonic treatment (with inversion). Minor-key mood and quaver motif also characterize the second theme of the orchestral introduction, hence dovetailing the thematic material and giving the whole with all its contrasts an inner unity. As sonorous an opening as the tutti of the movement has, so unobtrusively, as if improvising, does the soloist engage in the musical events, before virtuosically seizing the lead and formally setting out in the movement with the presentation of new motifs. The orchestra has in the process no mere accompanying function, but repeatedly structures the progress with short interjections and weighs in as an equal with what is thematic in the development sections, so that a lively dialogue emerges between orchestra

[3] *Mozart, Wolfgang Amadeus: Briefe und Aufzeichnungen*, ed. by the Internationale Stiftung Mozarteum Salzburg, compiled, with commentary, by Wilhelm A. Bauer and Otto Erich Deutsch, Vol.3 (Kassel, Basel, etc., 1963), 618
[4] *The Letters of Mozart and His Family*, trans. and ed. Emily Anderson, Vol.2, 2nd edition (New York, 1966), 902

and soloist. Mozart also shows his inclination to experiment when he assigns the soloist the actual principal theme only in the recapitulation and repeatedly 'titillates' the listener's ear with unexpected and unusual modulations. Despite its simplicity the second movement, an *Andante* with an abundance of melodic ideas, definitely stands at the centre of the concerto, with a somewhat playful, but very lyrical and eloquent style, as a strong expressive contrast to the animated first and last movements. What was merely sketch-like was certainly embellished by Mozart in performance and should also be understood nowadays as only 'scaffolding' to be filled out (e.g. bb59ff).

The theme of the rondo finale Mozart left quite unusually to the orchestra: the solo piano takes it over only after an extended, figurative couplet; this refrain is introduced by an elaborated 'entrance', that is, a mini-cadenza. An interlude in the minor is added, followed by a passage with the change of mode so typical of this concerto and with a striking dialogue between woodwinds as well as cello and solo piano. Further sections of refrain and couplet play with the thematic material and finally bring the concerto to a close in the sonorous key of the concerto beginning: no conventional virtuoso rondo, but a dramatically witty and musically clever conclusion to a sparkling composition. Mozart's son Franx Xaver also appreciated it and wrote for the first movement a cadenza that is still extant.

Mozart passed judgement on his own piano concertos, although a couple of years before the composition of the C major concerto, in a letter to his father of 23 December 1782:

these concertos are a happy medium between what is too easy and too difficult; they are very brilliant, pleasing to the ear, and natural without being vapid. There are passages here and there from which the connoisseurs alone can derive satisfaction; but these passages are written in such a way that the less learned cannot fail to be pleased, though without knowing why.[5]

– an assessment that also applies to the later concertos and has retained its validity up to today. 'In their perfection lies something incomprehensible', in the judgement of Manfred Hermann Schmid.[6]

Wolfgang Birtel
Translation: Margit L. McCorkle

[5] ibid., 833
[6] Manfred Hermann Schmid: *Orchester und Solist in den Konzerten von W. A. Mozart* (= Mozart Studies 9) (Tutzing, 1999), 8

VORWORT

Darf Johann Sebastian Bach als „Erfinder" des Cembalo-Konzertes angesehen werden, so gebührt Wolfgang Amadeus Mozart das Verdienst, das klassische Klavierkonzert geformt zu haben. Seine Konzerte gelten zu Recht als Höhepunkte der orchesterbegleiteten Solomusik, als Gipfelpunkt auch in Mozarts eigenem Œuvre:

Sein Ideal [der Konzertform] erreicht er doch erst in seinen Klavierkonzerten. Sie sind die Krönung und der Gipfel seines instrumentalen Schaffens überhaupt, zumindest auf dem Gebiete des Orchestralen,

urteilte einst Alfred Einstein.[1] Natürlich knüpfte Mozart an Vorbilder und Modelle an, etwa an Johann Christian Bach. Aus dessen Sonaten schuf er seine drei Klavierkonzerte, KV 107, weitere aus Klavierkompositionen anderer Komponisten – Vorübungen, Kompositionsstudien sozusagen. Mit dem D-Dur-Konzert, KV 175, legte er dann 1773 in Salzburg sein erstes eigenes Werk vor. Bis 1791 entstanden insgesamt 23 eigenständige Konzerte (eines davon für zwei, eines für drei Klaviere). Dazu kamen sieben weitere, eben die Bearbeitungen von Klaviersonaten Bachs und von Sonatensätzen anderer Komponisten, die sogenannten „Pasticcio"-Konzerte, sowie zwei Rondo-Einzelsätze als Final-Alternativen.

Voraussetzung für die Blüte der Klaviermusik in der Wiener Klassik waren die revolutionären Neuheiten im Instrumentenbau. Dank der Hammerklavier-Mechanik konnten Anschlag und Dynamik modifiziert werden – nach dem starren Cembaloklang eröffnete sich nun eine weite Welt der interpretatorischen Vielfalt. Und Mozart nutzte sie, um sich und seine Kunst ins rechte Licht zu setzen. Klavierkonzerte schrieb er in erster Linie für sich; gelegentlich wurden sie erst kurz vor der geplanten Aufführung fertig. So wundert es nicht, wenn Solopartien nur flüchtig notiert waren und später ergänzt oder geändert wurden.

Das Klavierkonzert Nr. 21 in C-Dur, KV 503, ist das erste der letzten drei großen Konzerte. Waren diese Opera zuvor in relativ rascher Folge entstanden, wurden sie in den letzten Lebensjahren seltener: Nach dem C-Dur-Konzert, Ende 1786, folgten nur noch 1788 das *Krönungskonzert* D-Dur, KV 537, und im Todesjahr 1791 das B-Dur-Werk, KV 595. Verwunderlich, nutzte doch Mozart diese Form, um sich in Subskriptionskonzerten als Instrumentalvirtuose zu präsentieren: Mit den „Akademien" während der Winter- und Fastenzeit empfahl er sich den einflussreichen Schichten in Wien als Klavierlehrer und Solist für Hauskonzerte und vermochte damit seine Einkünfte nicht unbeträchtlich zu steigern. Daneben versuchte sich Mozart in dieser Zeit auch als Opernkomponist zu etablieren. Mit der Premiere der *Hochzeit des Figaro* am 1. Mai 1786 konnte der Musiker hier einen entscheidenden Erfolg zunächst bei den Fachleuten, dann auch beim breiteren Publikum verbuchen. Nachdem während des Sommers die Kammermusik in den Vordergrund getreten war, beschäftigte sich Mozart dann zunächst wieder mit der Vorbereitung der traditionellen Winter-Akademie-Konzerte: Ein neues Klavierkonzert, eben dasjenige in C-Dur, KV 503, wurde vollendet, und der Komponist trug es am 4. Dezember 1786 in sein *Verzeichnüß aller meiner Werke*, ein: als „Ein klavier konzert. begleitung. 2 violini, 2 viole, 1 flauto, 2 oboe, 2 fagotti, 2 Corni, 2 Clarini, timpani e Baßo". Mozart hatte allerdings schon früher damit begonnen: Anfangstutti sowie Soloexposition entstanden bereits bis März 1785.[2]

Vier Abende waren zunächst geplant, wie Vater Leopold der Tochter Nannerl am 8. Dezember 1786 berichtete, Wolfgang gebe nämlich:

---

[1] Alfred Einstein: *Mozart. Sein Charakter, sein Werk*; zit. nach der Ausgabe: Frankfurt a. M. 1968, S. 302.

[2] Siehe Alan Tyson: *Mozart. Studies of the Autograph Scores*, Cambridge/MA, London 1987, S. 151f.

„auf dem Casin [Kasino] 4 Adventaccademien".[3] Doch die Planung von Subskriptionskonzerten geriet in den Hintergrund, denn Mozart reiste am 8. Januar 1787 überraschend nach Prag: „Dein Bruder wird itzt mit seiner Frau bereits in Prag seyn, denn er schreibt mir daß er verflossenen Montag dahin abreisen werde".[4] Nach drei Jahren „sinfonieloser" Zeit hatte Mozart noch auf die Schnelle eine neue Sinfonie fertiggestellt, in D-Dur, KV 504, die sogenannte *Prager*. Mehrere Wochen blieb der Komponist, und es scheint, dass er sich dort ein zweites „Standbein" sichern wollte: Der Auftrag für eine neue Oper war Frucht dieser Reise, und die Komposition des *Don Giovanni* sollte in den Mittelpunkt der kreativen Bemühungen des Jahres 1787 rücken. Selbst um die Konzerte zur Fastenzeit in Wien, die ihm normalerweise materielle Sicherheit brachten, konnte er sich nicht wie gewohnt kümmern. Das Interesse am Klavierkonzert, einer zentralen Gattung in Mozarts Schaffen, schwand.

Wenn es auch keinen direkten Nachweis darüber gibt, kann man davon ausgehen, dass Mozart das C-Dur-Konzert während einer der vier Dezember-Akademien 1786, vermutlich am 5. Dezember im Trattnerschen Kasino, erstmals spielte. Dass er es erst kurz vor der Aufführung fertigstellte, lässt den Arbeitsdruck ahnen, unter dem sich der Komponist befand. Sicherlich nahm Mozart die Neukomposition dann auch auf die Reise nach Prag mit. Einzig belegt ist allerdings nur eine Aufführung: Auf der Rückreise von Potsdam nach Wien gab Mozart am 12. Mai 1789 im Leipziger Gewandhaus eine Akademie, in der er neben dem B-Dur-Konzert, KV 456, auch dasjenige in C-Dur musizierte. Gedruckt wurde es zu Lebzeiten nicht; erst die Witwe Constanze gab es nach langer Planung und auf eigene Kosten 1797 im Eigenverlag heraus: gewidmet dem Prinzen Louis Ferdinand von Preußen, so das Titelblatt.

Das Klavierkonzert C-Dur, KV 503, ist Mozarts längstes Konzert (1. Satz: 432 Takte, 2. Satz: 109 Takte, 3. Satz: 382 Takte) und – wie die Werke dieser Gattung generell – dreisätzig angelegt. Virtuose Brillanz und ausgewogene formale Gliederung knüpfen stilistisch an die Konzerte in A-Dur, KV 488, und in c-Moll, KV 491, an. Doch die harmonische Gestaltung, das ständige Changieren zwischen Dur und Moll, das originelle Dialogisieren von Solo und Orchester, die starke kontrapunktische Durchdringung, der häufige Gebrauch des Orgelpunkts sowie der überquellende melodische Reichtum geben dem Werk eine ganz eigene Prägung. Die Orchestrierung mit doppelt besetzten Oboen, Fagotten und Hörnern nebst einer Flöte – auf die Mozart seit dem B-Dur-Konzert KV 450 nicht mehr verzichtete – und die für ein C-Dur-Konzert charakteristische Prägung durch Trompeten und Pauken geben dem Solowerk einen prachtvollen Rahmen. (Die Violen sind übrigens nicht, wie im eigenhändigen Verzeichnis angegeben, geteilt.)

Majestätisch, ja fast marschmäßig hebt das Allegro maestoso an, das sich formal als Verschmelzung von barocker Ritornell-Technik und klassischem Sonatenhauptsatz entpuppt. Schon gleich zu Beginn stellt Mozart mit Chromatik und Moll-Eintrübung die Weichen für eine sehr weiche, fließende und schillerndharmonische Durcharbeitung. Das immer wieder auftauchende Drei-Achtel-Auftakt-Motiv wird für den weiteren Verlauf konstituierend, ebenfalls die Kontrapunktik, auf die schon die kanonische Führung (mit Umkehrung) verweist. Moll-Stimmung und Achtel-Motiv bestimmen auch das zweite Thema der Orchestereinleitung, verzahnen somit das thematische Material und geben dem Ganzen, bei allem Kontrast, eine innere Einheitlichkeit. So klangvoll das Tutti den Satz eröffnet hat, so unauffällig, improvisatorisch klinkt sich der Solist in das musikalische Geschehen ein, ehe er mit virtuosem Zugriff die Führung übernimmt und mit der Präsentation neuer Motive den Satz formal aufbricht. Das Orchester hat dabei keine rein begleitende Funktion, sondern gliedert den Ablauf immer

[3] *Mozart, Wolfgang Amadeus: Briefe und Aufzeichnungen*, hrsg. von der Internationalen Stiftung Mozarteum Salzburg, ges. und erl. von Wilhelm A. Bauer und Otto Erich Deutsch, Bd. 3, Kassel, Basel usw. 1963, S. 618.
[4] Ebda., Bd. 4, Kassel, Basel usw. 1963, S. 7.

wieder mit kurzen Einwürfen und schaltet sich gleichberechtigt mit Thematischem in den Durchführungsteilen ein, so dass sich ein lebendiges Dialogisieren zwischen Orchester und Solist entwickelt. Die Lust am Experimentellen zeigt Mozart auch, wenn er dem Solisten das eigentliche Hauptthema erst bei der Reprise des Satzes zuweist und das Ohr des Zuhörers immer wieder mit überraschenden und ungewöhnlichen Modulationen „kitzelt". Trotz seiner Schlichtheit steht der zweite Satz, ein Andante, mit einer Fülle an melodischen Einfällen durchaus im Zentrum des Konzertes: mit etwas verspieltem, aber sehr lyrischem und beredtem Duktus, als ausdrucksstarker Kontrast zu den belebten Ecksätzen. Lediglich Skizzenhaftes wurde von Mozart sicherlich spielerisch ausgeziert, sollte auch heutzutage nur als „Gerüstsatz" verstanden und ausgestaltet werden (z. B. die Takte 59ff.). Das Thema des Final-Rondos überlässt Mozart ungewöhnlicherweise dem Orchester: Das Solo übernimmt es erst nach einem ausführlichem, figurativen Couplet; eingeleitet wird dieser Refrain von einem auskomponierten „Eingang", also einer Mini-Kadenz. Ein Moll-Zwischenspiel schließt sich an, gefolgt von einer Passage mit dem für dieses Konzert so typischen Wechsel der Tongeschlechter und mit einem aparten Dialog zwischen Holzbläsern sowie Violoncello und Soloklavier. Weitere Refrain- und Couplet-Abschnitte spielen mit dem thematischen Material und lassen das Konzert schließlich im klangvollen Ton des Konzertbeginns schließen: kein konventionelles Virtuosen-Rondo, sondern ein dramaturgisch geistreicher und musikalisch pfiffiger Abschluss einer fulminanten Komposition. Auch Mozarts Sohn Franz Xaver schätzte sie und schrieb für den ersten Satz eine Kadenz, die noch erhalten ist.

Mozart urteilte über seine eigenen Klavierkonzerte, wenn auch ein paar Jahre vor der Komposition des C-Dur-Konzertes, in einem Brief vom 28.12.1782 an den Vater:

die Concerten sind eben das Mittelding zwischen zu schwer, und zu leicht – sind sehr Brillant – angenehm in die ohren – Natürlich, ohne in das leere zu fallen – hie und da – können auch *kenner allein* satisfaction erhalten – doch so – daß die nicht=kenner damit zufrieden seyn müssen, ohne zu wissen warum.[5]

– eine Einschätzung, die auch auf die späteren Konzerte zutrifft und ihre Gültigkeit bis heute behalten hat: „In ihrer Vollkommenheit liegt etwas Unbegreifliches", urteilte der Musikforscher Manfred Hermann Schmid.[6]

Wolfgang Birtel

[5] Ebda., Bd. 3, Kassel, Basel usw. 1963, S. 245f.
[6] Manfred Hermann Schmid: *Orchester und Solist in den Konzerten von W. A. Mozart* (= Mozart Studien 9), Tutzing 1999, S. 8.

PIANO CONCERTO No. 25

Wolfgang Amadeus Mozart
(1756–1791)
K 503

I.

8

10

14

20

22

26

28

30

α) Ausführung analog Takt 124/125.

34

42

*) Kadenz

46

II.

48

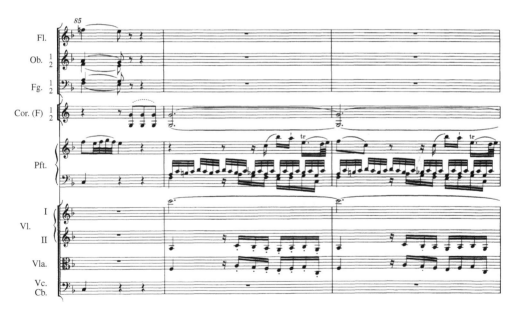

58

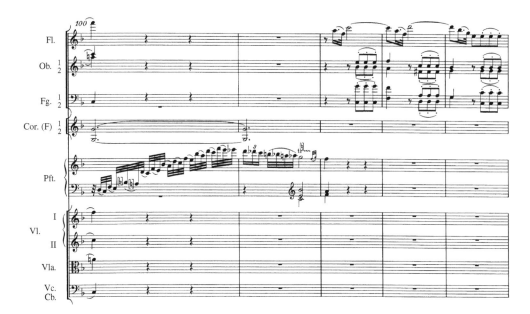

III.

62

*) Von Mozart selbst ausgeschriebener Eingang